"...his delight is in the law of the LORD; and in his law doth he meditate day and night."

Psalm 1:2

"Pray without ceasing."

1 Thessalonians 5:17

"A merry heart doeth good like a medicine..."

Proverbs 17:22

"But godliness with contentment is great gain."

1 Timothy 6:6

"Rejoice in the Lord, ye righteous; and give thanks at the remembrance of his holiness."

Psalm 97:12

"...the Lord is my helper, and I will not fear what man shall do unto me."

Hebrews 13:6

"... He that believeth on me hath everlasting life."

John 6:47

"...God hath given to us eternal life, and this life is in his Son."

1 John 5:11

"For ye are all the children of God by faith in Christ Jesus."

Galatians 3:26

"God is our refuge and strength, a very present help in trouble."

Psalm 46:1

"The fear of man bringeth a snare: but whoso putteth his trust in the Lord shall be safe."

Proverbs 29:25

"Glory ye in his holy name: let the heart of them rejoice that seek the LORD."

Psalm 105:3

"The Lord is good, a stronghold in the day of trouble; and he knoweth them that trust in him."

Nahum 1:7

"For thou wilt light my candle: the Lord my God will enlighten my darkness."

Psalm 18:28

"The Lord is my rock, and my fortress, and my deliverer;..."
Psalm 18:2

"...behold, I will pour out my spirit unto you, I will make known my words unto you."

Proverbs 1:23

"They that sow in tears shall reap in joy."

Psalm 126:5

"Enter into his gates with thanksgiving, and into his courts with praise: be thankful unto him, and bless his name."

Psalm 100:4

"Light is sown for the righteous, and gladness for the upright in heart."

Psalm 97:11

"These things I have spoken unto you, that my joy might remain in you, and that your joy might be full."

John 15:11

"Yet I will rejoice in the Lord, I will joy in the God of my salvation."

Habakkuk 3:18

"Seek the LORD, and his strength:
seek his face evermore."
Psalm 105:4

"For our heart shall rejoice in him, because we have trusted in his holy name."

Psalm 33:21

"...let the righteous be glad; let them rejoice before God:..."

Psalm 68:3

"...I will see you again, and your heart shall rejoice, and your joy no man taketh from you."

John 16:22

"I will not leave you comfortless: I will come to you."

John 14:18

"Beloved, if God so loved us, we ought also to love one another."

1 John 4:11

*"For he is our God: and we are the people of his pasture,
and the sheep of his hand..."*

Psalm 95:7

"...he loveth him that followeth after righteousness."

Proverbs 15:9

"Yea, I have loved thee with an everlasting love: therefore with loving kindness have I drawn thee."

Jeremiah 31:3

"We love him, because he first loved us."

1 John 4:19

"I love them that love me; and those that seek me early shall find me."

Proverbs 8:17

"The righteous cry, and the Lord heareth, and delivereth them out of all their troubles."

Psalm 34:17

"The eternal God is thy refuge, and underneath are the everlasting arms:..."

Deuteronomy 33:27

"Delight thyself also in the Lord: and he shall give thee the desires of thine heart."

Psalm 37:4

"With trumpets and sound of cornet make a joyful noise before the LORD, the King."

Psalm 98:6

"The Lord preserveth all them that love him..."

Psalm 145:20

"Grace be with all them that love our Lord Jesus Christ in sincerity..."

Ephesians 6:24

"Blessed are the meek: for they shall inherit the earth."

Matthew 5:5

"...they shall praise the Lord that seek him: your heart shall live for ever."

Psalm 22:26

"But he that shall endure unto the end,
the same shall be saved."

Matthew 24:13

"...Thy faith hath saved thee; go in peace."
Luke 7:50

"And all things, whatsoever ye shall ask in prayer, believing, ye shall receive."

Matthew 21:22

"Thou shalt make thy prayer unto him, and he shall hear thee, ..."

Job 22:27

"The Lord is far from the wicked: but he hearth the prayer of the righteous."

Proverbs 15:29

"Evening, and morning, and at noon, will I pray, and cry aloud: and he shall hear my voice."

Psalm 55:17

"Call unto me, and I will answer thee, and show thee great and mighty things, which thou knowest not."

Jeremiah 33:3

"The name of the Lord is a strong tower: the righteous runneth into it, and is safe."

Proverbs 18:10

"And who is he that will harm you, if ye be followers of that which is good?"

1 Peter 3:13

"The Lord is my light and my salvation;
whom shall I fear?..."

Psalm 27:1

"A good man obtaineth favour of the Lord..."

Proverbs 12:2

"So that a man shall say, Verily there is a reward for the righteous:..."

Psalm 58:11

"...and I will dwell in the house of the Lord for ever."

Psalm 23:6

"...ye shall search for me with all your heart."

Jeremiah 29:13

"The Lord is good unto them that wait for him, to the soul that seeketh him."

Lamentations 3:25

"Serve the LORD with gladness: come before his presence with singing."

Psalm 100:2

"For thus saith the Lord..., Seek ye me,
and ye shall live:..."
Amos 5:4

"Heal me, O Lord, and I shall be healed; save me, and I shall be saved: for thou art my praise."

Jeremiah 17:14

"By humility and the fear of the Lord are riches, and honour, and life."

Proverbs 22:4

"Wealth and riches shall be in his house: and his righteousness endureth for ever."

Psalm 112:3

"Trust in the Lord with all thine heart; and lean not unto thine own understanding."

Proverbs 3:5

"Casting all your care upon him; for he careth for you."

1 Peter 5:7

"Sing unto him, sing psalms unto him: talk ye of all his wondrous works."

Psalm 105:2

"Blessed is that man that maketh the Lord his trust,..."

Psalm 40:4

"... Be strong and of a good courage; be not afraid...for the Lord thy God is with thee whithersoever thou goest."

Joshua 1:9

"Thy word is a lamp unto my feet, and a light unto my path."

Psalm 119:105

"All the earth shall worship thee, and shall sing unto thee: they shall sing to thy name."

Psalm 66:4

"O come, let us worship and bow down: let us kneel before the Lord our maker."

Psalm 95:6

"Exalt the Lord our God, and worship at his holy hill; for the Lord our God is holy."

Psalm 99:9

"I will praise the Lord according to his righteousness:
and will sing praise to the name of the Lord most high."

Psalm 7:17

"For in the time of trouble he shall hide me in his pavilion:...he shall set me up upon a rock."

Psalm 27:5

"...but he loveth him that followeth after righteousness."

Proverbs 15:9

"Break forth into joy, sing together,...for the LORD hath comforted his people..."

Isaiah 52:9

"The blessings of the Lord, it maketh rich, and he addeth no sorrow with it."

Proverbs 10:22

"He hath made every thing beautiful in his time: also he hath set the world in their heart,..."

Ecclesiastes 3:11

"O clap your hands, all ye people; shout unto God with the voice of triumph."

Psalm 47:1

"The LORD is my shepherd; I shall not want."

Psalm 23:1

"My meditation of him shall be sweet: I will be glad in the LORD."

Psalm 104:34

"O give thanks unto the LORD; call upon his name: make known his deeds among the people."

Psalm 105:1

"Remember his marvellous works that he hath done; his wonders, and the judgments of his mouth;"

Psalm 105:5

"...I may dwell in the house of the LORD all the days of my life, to behold the beauty of the Lord..."

Psalm 27:4

"Wait on the LORD: be of good courage, and he shall strengthen thine heart: wait, I say, on the LORD."

Psalm 27:14

"The LORD is my strength and my shield; my heart trusted in him, and I am helped:..."

Psalm 28:7

"...I will sing unto the LORD, for he hath triumphed gloriously:..."

Exodus 15:1

"Make a joyful noise unto the LORD, all the earth: make a loud noise, and rejoice, and sing praise."

Psalm 98:4

"Every good gift and every perfect gift is from above, and cometh down from the Father of lights,..."

James 1:17

"Let the floods clap their hands: let the hills be joyful together."

Psalm 98:8

"Serve the LORD with gladness: come before his presence with singing."

Psalm 100:2

"O taste and see that the LORD is good: blessed is the man that trusteth in him."

Psalm 34:8

"Truly the light is sweet, and a pleasant thing it is for the eyes to behold the sun:"

Ecclesiastes 11:7

"He brought me to the banqueting house, and his banner over me was love."

Song of Solomon 2:4

"A friend loveth at all times..."

Proverbs 17:17

"Rejoice evermore."

1 Thessalonians 5:16

"For the LORD is great, and greatly to be praised:..."

Psalm 96:4

"Sing unto the LORD, bless his name; show forth his salvation from day to day."

Psalm 96:1-2

"And the peace of God, which passeth all understanding, shall keep your hearts and minds through Christ Jesus."

Phillipians 4:7

"O give thanks unto the LORD; for he is good: for his mercy endureth for ever."

Psalm 136:1

"...but as for me and my house, we will serve the LORD."

Joshua 24:15

"O sing unto the LORD a new song; for he hath done marvellous things:..."

Psalm 98:1

"The LORD make his face shine upon thee, and be gracious unto thee:"

Numbers 6:25

"And now abideth faith, hope, charity, these three; but the greatest of these is charity."

1 Corinthians 13:13

"Be of good courage, and he shall strengthen your heart, all ye that hope in the LORD."

Psalm 31:24

"But the LORD is my defense; and my God is the rock of my refuge."

Psalm 94:22

"Search me, O God, and know my heart: try me, and know my thoughts:"

Psalm 139:23

"I can do all things through Christ which strengtheneth me."

Philippians 4:13

"If ye abide in me, and my words abide in you, ye shall ask what ye will, and it shall be done unto you."

John 15:7

"Give ear to my words, O LORD, consider my meditation."

Psalm 5:1

"Rejoicing in hope; patient in tribulation; continuing instant in prayer;"

Romans 12:12

"Praise ye the LORD. O give thanks unto the LORD; for he is good: for his mercy endureth for ever."

Psalm 106:1

"...Make a joyful noise unto the LORD, all ye lands."

Psalm 100:1

"Sing unto him, sing psalms unto him: talk ye of all his wondrous works."

Psalm 105:2

"For the LORD is good; his mercy is everlasting; and his truth endureth to all generations."

Psalm 100:5

"As the Father hath loved me, so have I loved you: continue ye in my love."

John 15:9

*"The LORD lift up his countenance upon thee,
and give thee peace."*

Numbers 6:26

"...Man shall not live by bread alone, but by every word that proceedeth out of the mouth of God."

Matthew 4:5

"I will say of the Lord, He is my refuge and my fortress: my God; in him will I trust."

Psalm 91:2

"For he shall give his angels charge over thee, to keep thee in all thy ways."

Psalm 91:11

"... His compassions fail not. They are new every morning: great is thy faithfulness."

Lamentations 3:22-23

"I am Alpha and Omega, the beginning and the end, the first and the last."

Revelation 22:13

"To every thing there is a season, and a time to every purpose under the heaven:"

Ecclesaistes 3:1

"My fruit is better than gold...; and my revenue than choice silver."

Proverbs 8:19

"... And whosoever will, let him take the water of life freely."

Revelation 22:17

"...God is light, and in him is no darkness at all."

1 John 1:5

"I am the root and the offspring of David, and the bright and morning star."

Revelation 22:16

"Sing unto the LORD, all the earth; show forth from day to day his salvation."

1 Chronicles 16:23

"Draw nigh to God, and he will draw nigh to you..."

James 4:8

"... what doth the LORD require of thee, but to do justly, and to love mercy, and to walk humbly with thy God?"

Micah 6:8

"The LORD liveth; and blessed be my rock; and exalted be the God of the rock of my salvation."

2 Samuel 22:47